ASIAPAC COMIC

*The Message of
the Benevolent*

THE SAYINGS OF
CONFUCIUS
孔子說

Edited and illustrated by
Tsai Chih Chung

ASIAPAC • SINGAPORE

Publisher
ASIAPAC BOOKS PTE LTD
629 Aljunied Road
#04-06 Cititech Industrial Building
Singapore 389838
Tel: (65) 7453868
Fax: (65) 7453822
Email apacbks@singnet.com.sg

Visit us at our Internet home page
http://www.span.com.au/asiapac.htm

First published September 1994
Reprinted April1995, September 1996

© 1994 ASIAPAC BOOKS, SINGAPORE
ISBN 981-3029-40-4

Cover design by Marked Point Design
Typeset by Inscription Pte Ltd
Printed in Singapore by Loi Printing Pte Ltd

Publisher's Note

The Sayings of Confucius features the life of Confucius, selected sayings from *Lun Yu (The Analects)* and some of his more prominent pupils. In this revised edition, we give to readers a fuller discourse on *Lun Yu* or *The Analects*.

This new edition is a combination of two previous books, namely *The Sayings of Confucius* translated by Goh Beng Choo, and *Lun Yu – The Analects* translated by Mary Ng En Tzu.

Tsai Chih Chung has vividly depicted Confucius' life in a way to help you understand the renowned sage as a person, his philosophy and his teachings. This volume is especially helpful to those who wish to understand the humanity and moral values of the Chinese.

We feel honoured to have Tsai Chih Chung's permission to the translation rights to his best-selling comic series. Our thanks, too, to the translators Goh Beng Choo and Mary Ng En Tzu for their contributions which make this volume possible.

Publisher's Note

About the Editor/Illustrator

Tsai Chih Chung was born in 1948 in Chang Hwa County of Taiwan. He began drawing cartoon strips at the age of 17 and worked as Art Director for Kuang Chi Programme Service in 1971. He founded the Far East Animation Production Company and the Dragon Cartoon Production Company in 1976, where he produced two cartoon films entitled *Old Master Q* and *Shao Lin Temple*.

Tsai Chih Chung first got his four-box comics published in newspapers and magazines in 1983. His funny comic characters such as the Drunken Swordsman, Fat Dragon, One-eyed Marshal and Bold Supersleuth have been serialized in newspapers in Singapore, Malaysia, Taiwan, Hong Kong, Japan, Europe and the United States.

He was voted one of the Ten Outstanding Young People of Taiwan in 1985 and was acclaimed by the media and the academic circle in Taiwan.

The comic book *The Sayings of Zhuang Zi* was published in 1986 and marked a milestone in Tsai's career. Within two years, *Zhuang Zi* went into more than 72 reprints in Taiwan and 15 in Hong Kong and has to date sold over one million copies.

In 1987, Tsai Chih Chung published *The Sayings of Lao Zi, The Sayings of Confucius* and two books based on Zen. Since then, he has published more than 20 titles, out of which 10 are about ancient Chinese thinkers and the rest based on historical and literary classics. All these books topped the best-sellers' list at one time or another. They have been translated into other languages such as Japanese, Korean and Thai. Asiapac Books is the publisher for the English version of these comics.

Tsai Chih Chung can be said to be the pioneer in the art of visualizing Chinese literature and philosophy by way of comics.

Foreword

Confucius Was Human Too
On the comic book of "The Sayings of Confucius"

Confucius is the sage of China, and *The Analects* can be said to be the bible of China. It follows that the preachings of Confucius are a must in my series of Chinese philosophers in comics. In fact, *The Analects* came out top in the list of preferred publications named in the letters written by readers to me.

The Analects contains many beautiful phrases which have been widely quoted by people from all quarters through the ages. The preachings of Confucius have, for more than two thousand years, remained universally applicable. A significant one is his view that real knowledge comes from saying what one knows when one knows it and what one does not when one does not know it. It might be possible that, among his pupils, he had singled out Zi Lu to give this advice because Zi Lu was prone to weakness in this area. Yet how often and how common it is today for the people of our time to make the same mistake; people who do not know the truth behind things pretending that they do and even going on to make known their rather ludicrous views on these things!

Confucius was human too, and the most endearing quality of being human must surely be that touch of humanity and the ability to feel sad and happy, sorrowful and angry. Confucius sang when he was happy, showed his anger when he was angry, shed tears when he felt sad and was quick to rebuke and embarrass when things went wrong. He would occasionally crack a joke or two; he was successful in certain things he did, but failed in other things – he was not infallible like the gods. You may find his preachings more approachable if, after reading this book, you come to realize that Confucius was just like you and me.

There is a point which I would like to stress here. Right from the time when I started work on *The Sayings of Zhuang Zi*, I have given consideration to the problems of research. One example is the fact that brush and paper were not invented yet during the Spring and Autumn Period, neither were gold ingots used as money then. But if I were to illustrate the characters writing on bamboo strips (as the Chinese living in that age did), the reader might mistake them to be carving instead of writing. I have therefore decided to use symbols in depicting such things, bearing in mind that the aim of this series is to simplify ancient books rather than to engage in research. I hope you would understand and forgive me on this point.

Tsai Chih Chung
Taiwan

Contents

The Life of Confucius   1

Lun Yu — **The Analects**   45

I   **To Learn**（学而）   46

II   **To Govern**（为政）   54

III   **Eight Rows**（八佾）   64

IV   **To Live Among the Benevolent**（里仁）   68

V   **Gong Ye Zhang**（公治长）   82

VI   **Yong Ye**（雍也）   92

VII   **To Transmit**（述而）   99

VIII   **Count Tai**（泰伯）   113

IX   **Rarely Does the Master**（子罕）   116

X   **At Home**（乡党）   121

XI   **The Pioneers**（选进）   122

XII   **Yan Yuan**（颜渊）   125

XIII   **Zi Lu**（子路）   133

XIV   **Xian Enquires**（宪问）   140

XV   **Duke Ling of Wei**（卫灵公）   153

XVI   **Ji Family**（季氏）   167

XVII   **Yang Huo**（阳货）   172

XVIII   **The Viscount of Wei**（微子）   183

XIX   **Zi Zhang**（子张）   188

XX   **Yao Speaks**（尧曰）   196

Confucius' Pupils   197

    Yan Hui（颜回）   199

    Min Sun（闵损）   200

    Ran Yong（冉雍）   201

    Zhong You（仲由）   202

    Zai Yu（宰予）   203

    Duan Mu Ci（端木赐）   204

    Bu Shang（卜商）   205

    Tantai Mie Min（澹台灭明）   206

    Yuan Xian（原宪）   207

    Zhuan Sun Shi（颛孙师）   208

    Zeng Shen（曾参）   209

    Fan Xu（樊须）   210

    You Ruo（有若）   211

    Gong Ye Zhang（公冶长）   212

    Nan Gong Gua（南宫括）   213

    Gong Xi Chi（公西赤）   214

Epilogue   215

The Life
of
Confucius

Kong Qiu, also Kong Zhongni, was born around
551 BC. He is more commonly known as Confucius.

The Life of Confucius

Confucius was born in Chang Ping Village of the state of Lu, during King Ling of Zhou's twenty-first year in reign (551 BC).

Confucius' father was Kong Shu Liang He, a mighty man of ten *chi* tall. He had nine daughters by his wife and a son by his concubine, but the boy was unfortunately handicapped.

After the age of sixty-four, Shu Liang He married Madam Yuan, who bore him Confucius.

When Confucius was three, his father passed away.

As a child, Confucius loved to lay out the different sacrificial vessels to play.

He would imitate the rituals and gestures of adults at ceremonies.

When Confucius was fifteen, his mind became fixed on learning.

7

All the age of nineteen, he married Yuan Guan from the state of Song.

8

The following year, they had a son and named him Kong Li, meaning 'carp'.

10

At the age of twenty, Confucius worked as a clerk at the granaries.

11

He was noted for his accuracy and preciseness in keeping accounts.

Later he was made overseer of the flocks and grazing grounds. The flocks were so well tended that they flourished.

12

Years later, he worked as a foreman of building constructions.

13

14 In the twentieth year of Duke Zhao's reign of the state of Lu...

15 Nan Gong Jing Shu recommended Confucius for studies of the rites in the state of Zhou.

16 While studying the rites in Zhou, Confucius visited Lao Zi to consult him in this field.

17 Upon completing the course, Lao Zi said to him:

The rich offer material goods as parting gifts; the benevolent offer words. I'm no rich man, so let me give you a few lines.

18 An intelligent man always gets into trouble because he loves to discuss about others; a learned man is always in peril because he exposes the faults of others. Children must have their parents at heart, subjects must have their kings at heart and not just care only for themselves.

In the year when Confucius was thirty-five, three counsellors of the Lu State teamed up to attack Duke Zhao, who fled to the state of Qi in defeat.

25

Not long afterwards, Confucius also left for Qi when revolts again broke out in Lu.

26

Then Confucius planned to use his connections with Gao Zhao Zi, a high official in Qi, to gain access to Duke Jing, and for that, he went to work as a steward for Zhao Zi's family.

27

28

Having heard the Shao music, Confucius set to learn it for three months. He was so engrossed in it that he could not tell the taste of meat.

29

It's amazing how music can bring one to such heights.

6

30 During the Spring and Autumn Period, the states were in shambles. The rulers did not behave like rulers and subjects did not behave like subjects.

Duke Zhao was eventually defeated and expelled by Ji Sun.

31 And Duke Jing of Qi was under the control of Chen Heng, who was so powerful that it seemed he could usurp Duke Jing's position any time.

So, when Duke Jing asked Confucius about the formula for good government, Confucius answered:

32 Let the ruler be like a ruler, the subject be like a subject, the father be like a father, and the son be like a son.

33 Right, if people do not behave in the manners befitting their positions, even if there is grain, would we get to eat it in peace?

What is the principle of governing then?

The most important thing about governing is to use your resources wisely and curb your excesses.

34

35 I want to give my land at Ni Xi to Confucius.

Duke Zhao was forced into exile and wandered for seven years. He died outside his state and Duke Ding succeeded the throne.

42

But Duke Ding was powerless and the state was controlled by the three families of Ji, Shu and Meng.

43

Ji Sun, who was at the helm in Lu, was in turn terrorised into obedience by Yang Huo, a steward of his house.

44

45

In the fifth year of the reign of Duke Ding, Yang Huo staged a revolt and seized power from Ji Sun.

46 He terrorised Duke Ding into obedience, sent his opponents into exile and became dictator of Lu.

47

With no desire to serve a government which violated the rites, Confucius retired to concentrate on the study of *Shu* (History), *Shi* (The Odes), *Li* (Rites) and *Yue* (Music).

9

In the eighth year of Duke Ding's reign, Yang Huo decided to remove the three families from power. 55

Destroy the three families! I shall replace them!

Yes, Your Highness!

56 The three families fought tooth-and-nail to safeguard their power.

57

Yang Huo was defeated by them and he fled to Qi.

Yang Huo's failure gave Confucius an opportunity to take part in governmental affairs.

58

Ji Sun admired Confucius greatly for not pandering to Yang Huo. He recommended Confucius to Duke Ding of Lu. 59

60 Duke Ding made Confucius governor of the middle district of Lu.

11

Confucius, who was in office for only a year, was so efficient that officials of the neighbouring estates modelled their policies after his.

61

62 Confucius was further promoted to the rank of Minister of Public Works and then to that of Police Commissioner to keep law and peace.

63

During those years, the criminals and illegal traders of Lu either turned over a new leaf or left the state on their own.

Because Confucius moved the people with virtue and educated them with rites, everyone in Lu respected the elderly.

64

65

The men and women of Lu walked at a distance from each other. Things left behind by owners were never picked up and at night, doors were left unlocked without fear of robbery.

I have heard that civil affairs are accompanied by armament and military affairs are accompanied by civil rites.

72

Whenever the ancient lords stepped over their borders, they brought along their official retinue. Please bring with you the Marshals of the Left and the Right.

Fine.

73

74

Duke Ding brought with him Confucius and the Marshals of the Left and the Right to the meeting at Jia Gu.

75

The two princes met at Jia Gu and exchanged formalities.

93 Execute them!

94 Duke Jing was moved by the stern countenance of Confucius.

95 After returning to Qi, he felt uneasy.

The Prince of Lu is assisted by the rites of the gentleman, while you guys peddled to me the ways of the barbarian. What shall I do?

96 If a gentleman made a mistake, he apologises with action. A petty man apologises with words. Maybe fulfilling the pact may put Your Majesty at ease.

97 All right. I shall return the occupied lands to Lu as a token of apology.

Yes, Your Majesty.

18

In the summer of the twelfth year of Duke Ding's reign...

I hope to return military power to the state. I suggest tearing down the city walls in the three family estates.

Fine.

98

I intend to tear down the walls in the three estates to prevent another Yang Huo affair.

99

It's better to tear down the city walls, otherwise the vassals might use their cities as bases for military revolts.

100

Shu Sun went ahead to destroy the wall of the Hou family.

101

I command you to withdraw your troops from Fei because I'm going to destroy the city wall.

102

How disgusting! Ji Sun intends to destroy our bases. What shall we do?

That's terrible! He is afraid of our force.

103

21

22

120 Duke Jing of Qi got worried upon news about the smooth running of Lu.

If Confucius continues to be in charge, Lu will become the supreme state. Since we are the nearest to them, our land will be the first to be annexed.

Let's sabotage their reforms and pick some beauties for Prince Lu.

121

Yes, that's a good idea.

122

123 So Qi presented eighty beauties and one hundred and twenty horses to the Prince of Lu.

124 Duke Jing has sent us beauties and horses. They are stationed at the High Gate on the south.

125 Let's have a look at them.

Since then, Duke Ding and Ji Sun indulged themselves in pleasure-seeking and did not attend to official duties for three days.

126

At the sacrificial feast, they did not give the counsellors sacrificial meat in accordance with the rites.

127

Let's leave this place.

Yes, let's go.

128

Now that Yang Huo's supporters have been wiped out, Ji Sun's position is stable, I wouldn't be of any use any more. Besides, the prince has no real power... Let's go.

129

130

Thereafter Confucius resigned and left Lu to go to Wei.

24

27

153
All the princes who are on friendly terms with our prince must meet our Lady Nan Zi. The Lady wishes to see you too.

That's fine.

154
What's so exciting about meeting this kind of woman?

155
After entering the door, Confucius bowed politely toward the north, while Lady Nan Zi bowed in return behind a curtain. Zi Lu was terribly annoyed.

156
I had no intention of meeting her, but since circumstances forced me to, I had to return her respects.

Humph!

157
If I have done something improper, let Heaven punish me, let Heaven punish me!

29

158
After a month or so, Duke Ling and Lady Nan Zi went on a city tour in a chariot, with Confucius following behind in the second chariot.

159
How pretty!
How beautiful!
What a beauty!

160
I'm yet to come across men who love virtues as ardently as they love beauties.

161
So disappointed was he that he finally left Wei to travel to Cao.

162
That year, Duke Ding passed away.

32

174 Confucius arrived at Chen.

175 He stayed in Si Cheng Zhen Zi's house for three years.

176 Just then the state of Jin and the state of Chu were fighting for power and more than once they attacked Chen.

177 Even the state of Wu encroached on the territory of Chen.

178 Go home! Go home! The boys who remain home are brilliant, only that they are not cautious. Nevertheless, they are go-getters who never forget their roots.

So said, Confucius left Chen.

185 Forget the promise. Head straight for Wei.

186 Master, can one go back on one's promises?

187 A deal made under threats is not something which Heaven shall approve of.

188 Duke Ling was pleased to hear about Confucius' arrival, and he went personally to receive him at the Gate.

189 What a pity! I'm old and I cannot offer you a post.

190 Sigh!

191 If someone were to leave the running of the state to me, I shall have something to show him within a year and produce tangible results in three years.

192
On one occasion, Duke Ling asked Confucius about military tactics...

I know something about sacrificial rites, but nothing about military affairs.

194 The following day, while Duke Ling and Confucius were having a conversation, a flight of wild geese flew past and caught the glance of the Duke, who paid no attention to what Confucius was saying.

195
The Master decided to leave Wei to go to Chen.

196
The next year he went from Chen to Cai.

Confucius turned sixty-eight in the eleventh year of the reign of Duke Ai and Ji Kang Zi set off to welcome him back to Lu with pompous ceremony.

208

It had been fourteen years since Confucius left Lu to travel among the states.

209

Although Duke Ai and Ji Kang Shi did seek Confucius' advice on government matters, the Master's ideas were never put to use.

210

No longer hoping for an official post, Confucius stayed home a good deal of time to edit The Odes (*Shi Jing*), compile the ancient music and rites, preserve the I *Ching* and edit the Spring and Autumn Annals.

周易
春秋
礼乐
诗书

211

He usually lectured at the spot between River Zhu and River Si to impart his knowledge to his pupils.

213

He would accept all people — be they poor or rich — and coached them according to their abilities.

Confucius founded four subjects on **Culture, Conduct, Loyalty** and **Trustworthiness.**

文行忠信

214

215

He set up eight principles of learning, self-cultivation and social relationship. These are: To investigate things;
To expand our knowledge;
To be sincere;
To rectify one's mind;
To cultivate oneself;
To regulate one's family;
To manage the state; and
To bring peace to the world.

格 致 诚 正 修 齐 治 平
物 知 意 心 身 家 国 天
下

216

Thereafter one should proceed to learn the Rites, Music, Archery, Horsemanship, History and Mathematics, to reach the three virtues of **Wisdom, Benevolence** and **Courage.**

217 Confucius divided his teachings into four stages:
to set one's mind on The Way;
to base oneself on virtue;
to rely on benevolence for support; and
to seek recreation in the arts.

志　据　依　游
于　于　于　于
道　德　仁　艺

Literature.

Government.

On his list of priorities, **Conduct** is the first requirement, **Speech** comes second, **Government Matters** third and **Literature** last.

Language.

Virtue.

218

41

42

224 Seven days later, Confucius passed away.

225 He died in the fourth lunar month in the sixteenth year of Duke Ai, at the age of seventy-three.

226

The historian Si Ma Qian said:

These lines appear in The Odes:
Majestic indeed is the mountain that we look up to;
Great indeed is the virtue that we seek to emulate.

As a commoner, Confucius' teachings were sustained for more than a thousand years. There is no intellectual who does not regard him as his spiritual mentor. Confucius is indeed the supreme sage!

论 语

LUN YU – The Analects

Book I, Chapter 1
To Learn

学而时习之，不亦说乎？有朋自远方来，不亦乐乎？人不知而不愠，不亦君子乎？

学而第一：一

Isn't it a joy to acquire knowledge and be able to put it to use?

1

Isn't it a great pleasure to have a friend visiting from afar?

2

Isn't he a gentleman who bears no grudge against those who do not know his strength?

3

Book I, Chapter 2
To Learn

有子曰：「其为人也孝弟，而好犯上者鲜矣。不好犯上，而好作乱者，未之有也。君上务本，本立而道生。孝弟也者，其为仁之本与？」

学而第一：二

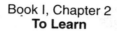

A disciple of Confucius, You Zi, said:

A man who is filial to his parents and respects his elder brothers is seldom disposed to quarrel with his superiors.

1

He who is not disposed to quarrel with his superiors will not be disposed to stir up chaos and create confusion.

2

The superior man devotes his attention to work on what is fundamental in life. When this is firmly established, The Way is naturally conceived.

3

Filial piety and fraternal respect – these are indeed the foundations and roots of virtue and benevolence!

4

47

Book I, Chapter 4
To Learn

曾子曰：「吾日三省吾身：
为人谋，而不忠乎？与朋友
交，而不信乎？传，不习
乎？」

学而第一：四

Zeng Zi said:

Every day I examine myself on three things:

Have I done my best in doing things for another man?

Have I been trustworthy in my dealings with friends?

Have I failed to revise what the Master had taught me?

Book I, Chapter 5
To Learn

子曰：「道千乘之国，
敬事而信，节用而爱
人，使民以时。」

学而第一：五

Confucius said:

To rule a country with a thousand war chariots, one must give serious attention to government, gain the people's trust,

Exercise economy in expenditure, love the people,

And employ labour at the proper time.

Book I, Chapter 6
To Learn

子曰：「弟子入则孝，出则弟，谨而信，泛爱众，而亲仁，行有余力，则以学文。」

学而第一：六

Confucius said: A young man should be filial when he is at home;

1

2

Respect his elders when he is abroad;

3

Be careful in his deeds and truthful in his speech;

4

Love all men, and seek friendship with virtuous men.

5

When he has done all these, then let him study the polite arts*.

*the polite arts — not merely literary studies, but also all the accomplishments of a gentleman: ceremonies, music, archery, horsemanship, writing and arithmetic.

Book I, Chapter 8
To Learn

子曰：「君子不重则不威，学则不固。主忠信，无友如己者，过则勿惮改。」

学而第一：八

If a scholar is frivolous, he will not command the respect of men.

You must study hard and learn discipline.

Yes! Yes! Hee! Hee!

Also, his learning will be shallow. It cannot be solid and profound.

A person must not have friends who are not like himself.

Also, he must not be afraid to correct his faults.

子曰：「不患
人之不己知，
患 不 知 人
也。」
学而第一： 十六

Confucius said:

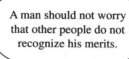

A man should not worry that other people do not recognize his merits.

He should only worry that he has failed to recognize the merits of other people.

53

Book II, Chapter 1
To Govern

为政以德。譬如北辰，
居其所，而众星共之。
为政第二：一

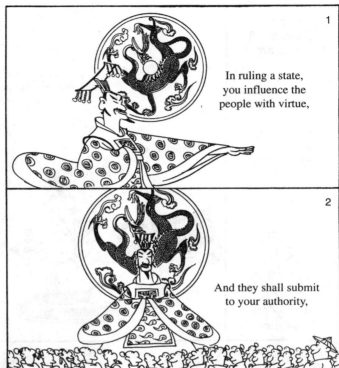

1

In ruling a state,
you influence the
people with virtue,

2

And they shall submit
to your authority,

3

Which is similar to the Polar
Star which stays put while the
other stars move around it.

Book II,
Chapter 3
To Govern

子曰：「道之以政，齐
之以刑，民免而无耻；
道之以德，齐之以礼，
有耻且格。」

为政第二：三

Confucius said: If people are governed by laws, and order is maintained through punishment, then people will keep away from wrongdoing; but only because they want to avoid punishment, not because they have a sense of shame in doing wrong.

We'd better not commit any crime for we'll be heavily punished if we're caught...

Won't it be great if criminals aren't punished?

If people are inspired by a moral and virtuous government, and order is maintained by rites of propriety, then people will want to be good because they have a sense of shame in dong wrong.

Committing crimes is shameful; let's mend our ways.

Alright!

Book II, Chapter 4
To Govern

吾十有五而志于学；三十而立；四十而不惑；五十而知天命；六十而耳顺；七十而从心所欲，不踰矩。

为政第二：四

1

When I was fifteen, I set my mind on learning,

2

At thirty, I held on firmly to what I've learned.

3

At forty, I knew all about managing affairs and understanding truth.

4

At fifty, I realized that Heaven had its own will. I blamed neither Heaven nor man.

5

At sixty, I could tell whether a man was telling the truth and judge his character by listening to his speech.

6

At seventy, I could follow my heart's wishes and not make mistakes.

Book II, Chapter 7
To Govern

子游问孝。子曰：「今
之孝者，是谓能养。至
于犬马，皆能有养。不
敬，何以别乎？」
为政第二：七

Zi You asked about filial piety and Confucius said:

Nowadays, the duty of a good son is only to make sure that his parents get enough to eat;

1

2

Even dogs and horses are likewise cared for...

3

If there is only care without respect, what is the difference between caring for your parents and looking after the dogs and horses?

Book II, Chapter 11
To Govern

子曰：「温故而知
新，可以为师
矣。」
为政第二：十一

Book II, Chapter 13
To Govern

子贡问君子。子曰：「先行其言，而后从之。」
为政第二：十三

Zi Gong asked Confucius about the nature of the superior man. Confucius said:

The superior man acts before he speaks; his words follow his actions,

1

2

And afterwards, he speaks only according to what he has done.

Book II, Chapter 14
To Govern

子曰：「君子周而
不比，小人比而不
周。」
为政第二：十四

1

Confucius said:
The superior man is
impartial and is not biased.

2

The petty man is prejudiced.

Book II, Chapter 15
To Govern

子曰：「学而不思
则罔，思而不学则
殆。」

为政第二：十五

Confucius said: Reading and studying without thinking is futile labour;

1

2

What a book-worm!

And thinking without reading and studying is perilous.

3

Nonsense!

4

61

Book II,
Chapter 16
To Govern

子曰：「攻乎异
端，斯害也已。」
为政第二：十六

Book II,
Chapter 17
To Govern

子曰：「由，诲
女，知之乎？知之
为知之，不知为不
知，是知也。」
为政第二：十七

1 Zhong You, do you understand all that I have taught you?

2 If you understand, say that you understand.

3 If you do not, say that you do not.

4 Such is what knowledge is about.

63

Book III,
Chapter 7
Eight Rows

子曰：「君子无所争，
必也射乎！揖让而升，
下而饮，其争也君
子。」

八佾第三：七

Confucius said:

The superior man has no contentions. For him, if there is any kind of striving, it is, perhaps, in archery.

Before the contest, he bows to his rival...

Then he rises to compete;

After the contest, he comes down and bows again to his rival,

The loser is made to drink wine as his forfeit. This is how superior men contend with one another.

Book III, Chapter 15
Eight Rows

子入大庙，每事问。或曰：
「孰谓鄹人之子知礼乎？入
大庙，每事问。」子闻之
曰：「是礼也！」

八佾第三：十五

When Confucius first entered the temple of the Duke of Zhou to assist with making sacrifices, he asked questions about everything.

Who said that the son of the man from Zhou knows about rites? He asks questions about everything in the temple.

To ask questions about everything in a modest manner is to know the proper rite.

Book III, Chapter 17
Eight Rows

子贡欲去告朔之饩羊。
子曰：「赐也！尔爱其
羊，我爱其礼。」
八佾第三：十七

Zi Gong wanted to do away with the sacrificial sheep usually offered at the announcement of the new moon.

1

Master, please cut out the sacrificial sheep.

2

Ci, you wouldn't part with the cost of the sheep,

but I wouldn't part with the sacrificial rites.

3

66

定公问：「君使
臣，臣事君，如之
何？」孔子对曰：
「君使臣以礼，臣
事君以忠。」
八佾第三：十九

Duke Ding asked:

How should a ruler employ and use his ministers, and how should ministers serve their ruler?

1

Let the ruler use his ministers according to the rules of propriety,

Propriety.

2

Let the ministers serve their ruler with loyalty.

Loyalty.

3

67

To Live Among the Benevolent

子曰：「不仁者，不可
以久处约，不可以长处
乐。仁者安仁；知者利
仁。」
里仁第四：二

Why should I put up with such poverty and hardship?

Confucius said:
A man without virtue cannot endure adversity for long.

1

Nor can he enjoy prosperity for long.

Why should I be contented with only such enjoyment?

A man of virtue rests content in Virtue;

2　3

A man of wisdom recognizes the benefits that Virtue brings.

4

Book IV, Chapter 3
To Live Among the Benevolent

子曰：「唯仁
者，能好人，
能恶人。」
里仁第四：三

Confucius said:

Only a virtuous man can rightly love;

"Goodness"

Or rightly hate.

"Wickedness"

Book IV, Chapter 4
To Live Among the Benevolent

子曰：「苟志于仁
矣，无恶也。」
里仁第四：四

Confucius said:
If a man sets his mind
to be virtuous...

Goodness

1

2

He will not practise wickedness.

Goodness

71

Book IV, Chapter 8
To Live Among the Benevolent

子曰：「朝聞道，
夕死可矣！」
里仁第四：八

Book IV, Chapter 9
To Live Among the Benevolent

士志于道，而耻恶
衣恶食者，未足与
议也。

里仁第四：九

If a gentleman has set his mind on seeking The Way,

1

Yet still feels ashamed of wearing shabby clothes and...

2

Eating lousy food,

3

There is no point in discussing The Way with him.

4

Book IV, Chapter 10
To Live Among the Benevolent

子曰：「君子之于天下也，无适也，无莫也，义之与比。」
里仁第四：十

1

Confucius said:

In his dealings with the world, the superior man is not invariably set on what is or is not permitted;

2

"Righteousness"

He will just follow whatever is right.

Book IV, Chapter 12
To Live Among the Benevolent

子曰：「放于
利而行，多
怨。」
里仁第四：十二

Confucius said:

He who acts only with a view to his own advantage...

Surely makes many enemies and invites much hatred.

Book IV,
Chapter 14
**To Live
Among the
Benevolent**

不患无位，患所以
立。不患莫己知，
求为可知也。
里仁第四：十四

Do not worry that
you have no
position,

Worry that you may not
have the necessary
qualifications.

1

Do not worry that
you are not being
discovered.

Ask yourself what it is you
have that is worthy of
people's recognition.

3

4

**Book IV,
Chapter 16
To Live
Among the
Benevolent**

子曰：「君子
喻于义，小人
喻于利。」
里仁第四：十六

Confucius said:
The superior man
understands righteousness,

As long as it is
right, I will do it
even at the cost
of my life.

The petty man
understands only gain.

As long as it
benefits me, I
will do it.

Book IV,
Chapter 17
**To Live Among
the Benevolent**

见贤思齐焉，
见不贤而内自
省也。
里仁第四：十七

Book IV,
Chapter 19
**To Live
Among the
Benevolent**

父母在，不远
游；游必有
方。
里仁第四：十九

1

When your parents are alive, you should not travel far,

2

If you must do so, you should always tell them your whereabouts to save them the anguish of worrying for you.

Book IV, Chapter 22
To Live Among the Benevolent

子曰：「古者
言之不出，耻
躬之不逮
也。」
里仁第四：二二

Confucius said:

In the old days, the ancients did not speak readily,

Because they would be ashamed if their actions did not match their words.

I talk about it but I cannot do it. How shameful!

Book IV, Chapter 25
To Live Among the Benevolent

德不孤，必有邻。
里仁第四：二五

A virtuous man is never lonely.

Others who are as virtuous as he is
are bound to be drawn to him.

Book V, Chapter 8
Gong Ye Zhang

子謂子貢曰：「女與回也孰愈？」對曰：「賜也何敢望回！回也聞一以知十，賜也聞一以知二。」子曰：「弗如也，吾與女如也。」

公冶長第五：八

Confucius said to Zi Gong:

Between you and Yan Hui, who do you think is more capable?

1

How can I be compared with Yan Hui?

2

3

When Yan Hui is told one thing, he understands ten.

When I am told one thing, I understand only two.

Yes, you are not as capable as Yan Hui. Neither of us is as capable as he is.

Book V, Chapter 9
Gong Ye Zhang

宰予昼寝。子曰：「朽木不可雕也，粪土之墙，不可朽也。于予与何诛！」子曰：「始吾于人也，听其言而信其行；今吾于人也，听其言而观其行。于予与改是！」
公冶长第五：九

1
Zai Yu was in bed during the day.

2
A block of rotten wood cannot be carved, nor can a soiled wall be white-washed.

3
What is the use of rebuking someone like Zai Yu?

4
I used to believe that men practised what they said;

5
Now I observe their action to see if it matches with what they have said. My view has changed because of Zai Yu.

Book V, Chapter 10
Gong Ye Zhang

子曰：「吾未见刚者！」或对曰：「申枨。」子曰：「枨也欲，焉得刚？」

公治长第五：十

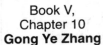

84

Book V, Chapter 14
Gong Ye Zhang

子贡问曰：「孔文子何以谓
之文也?」子曰：「敏而好
学，不耻下问，是以谓之文
也。」

公冶长第五：十四

Why was Kong Wen Zi called 'Wen'?

Zi Gong asked:

1

He was bright and eager to learn,

2

He did not feel ashamed to seek the advice of people who were beneath him in rank.

3

For this reason, he was called 'Wen'.

4

Book V, Chapter 15
Gong Ye Zhang

子谓：「子产有君
子之道四焉：其行
己也恭，其事上也
敬，其养民也惠，
其使民也义。」

公冶长第五：十五

1

Zi Chan possesses four characteristics of the superior man...

Confucius said:

2

In conducting himself, he is courteous and humble;

3

In serving his superior, he is respectful and sincere;

4

In caring for the needs of the people, he is generous and kind;

5

In employing the services of the people, he is just and fair.

86

Book V, Chapter 22 **Gong Ye Zhang**

子曰：「伯夷、
叔齐，不念旧
恶，怨是用
希。」
公冶长第五：二二

Confucius said:

Bo Yi and Shu Qi did not keep in mind the wrongs that others had done to them.

1

2

Therefore few were the resentments directed against them.

Oh yes!

They're really like saints, aren't they?

Book V, Chapter 24
Gong Ye Zhang

巧言、令色、足
恭，左丘明耻
之，丘亦耻之。
匿怨而友其人，
左丘明耻之，丘
亦耻之。

公冶长第五：二四

1 To utter sweet words, display ingratiating manners and be overly humble.

2 These are conducts Zuo Qiu Ming considered shameful. I, too, find them shameful.

3 To bear hatred towards someone while being superficially friendly...

4 This, Zuo Qiu Ming found shameful. I, too, find it shameful.

Book V, Chapter 25
Gong Ye Zhang

颜渊、季路侍。子曰：「盍各言尔志?」子路曰：「愿车马、衣轻裘，与朋友共，敝之而无憾。」颜渊曰：「愿无伐善，无施劳。」子路曰：「愿闻子之志!」子曰：「老者安之，朋友信之，少者怀之。」

公冶长第五：二五

89

**Book V,
Chapter 26
Gong Ye
Zhang**

子曰：「已矣
乎！吾未能见其
过，而内自讼者
也。」
公冶长第五：二六

Confucius said:

> Alas!
> Alas!

> I have yet to see a man who can perceive his own faults and reproach himself.

Book V,
Chapter 27
Gong Ye Zhang

十室之邑，必
有忠信如丘者
焉，不如丘之
好学也。

公冶长第五：二七

Within the hamlet of only
ten families,

1

2

It is not difficult to find
someone as conscientious
and trustworthy as I,

But only that he may
not possess as much
love for learning.

3

Book VI, Chapter 3
Yong Ye

哀公问：「弟子孰为好
学？」孔子对曰：「有颜回
者好学：不迁怒，不贰过。
不幸短命死矣！今也则亡，
未闻好学者也。」

雍也第六：三

Book VI, Chapter 16
Yong Ye

子曰：「质胜
文则野；文胜
质则史。文质
彬彬，然后君
子。」

雍也第六：十六

Confucius said:

Where natural qualities exceed education, you get a rough village rustic;

Where education exceeds natural qualities, you get a pedantic clerk.

1

2

It is only where natural qualities and education are balanced that you get the true superior man.

3

Book VI, Chapter 18
Yong Ye

子曰：「知之
者不如好之
者，好之者不
如乐之者。」
雍也第六：十八

Book VI, Chapter 21
Yong Ye

知者乐水，仁者乐山。知者动，
仁者静。知者乐，仁者寿。

雍也第六：二一

The wise, being enlightened, likes free-flowing water.

1

2

The benevolent, being rational, loves sturdy mountains.

The wise is active.

3

4

The benevolent is quiet.

5

The wise delights in himself.

6

The benevolent lives a long, serene life.

96

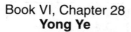

Book VI, Chapter 28
Yong Ye

子贡曰：「如有博施于民，而能济众，何如？可谓仁乎？」子曰：「何事于仁，必也圣乎！尧舜其犹病诸！夫仁者，已欲立而立人，已欲达而达人。能近取譬，可谓仁之方也已。」

雍也第六：二八

Suppose a man universally bestows kindness on people and can really help the multitude. Would you say that such a man is morally virtuous?

Zi Gong asked Confucius:

1

He is not just a virtuous man, he's a saint! Indeed, his achievements transcend even the works of Yao and Shun!

2

Who is virtuous? A man who knowing his own desire to be established, will help others to establish themselves; and knowing his own desire to attain success, will help others to attain success.

3

In fact, to consider others by what is in ourselves is the way of Virtue.

4

Book VII, Chapter 1
To Transmit

述而不作，信而好古，
窃比于我老彭。
述而第七：一

I transmit but do not create,

I believe firmly in the ways of the ancient kings and have a love for the ancient culture.

I emulate the fine example of Old Peng of the Shang Dynasty.

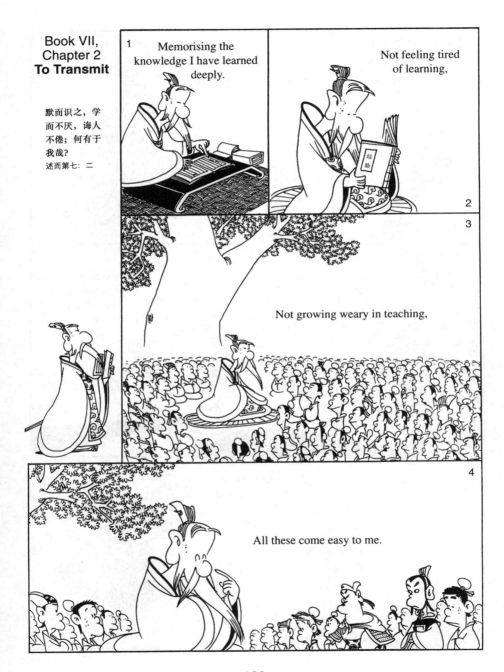

Book VII,
Chapter 2
To Transmit

默而识之，学
而不厌，诲人
不倦；何有于
我哉?
述而第七：二

1 Memorising the knowledge I have learned deeply.

Not feeling tired of learning,

2

3 Not growing weary in teaching,

4 All these come easy to me.

Book VII,
Chapter 5
To Transmit

甚矣吾衰也!
久矣，吾不复
梦见周公!
述而第七：五

**Book VII,
Chapter 6
To Transmit**

志于道，据于
德，依于仁，
游于艺。
述而第七：六

1

A man should set his
sight on The Way,

2

Base his conduct
on virtue,

德

3

Be guided by benevolence
in living and finally,

4

Take recreation
in the arts.

Book VII,
Chapter 7
To Transmit

自行束修以
上，吾未尝无
诲焉!
述而第七：七

To anyone who offers any gift
in respect of the teacher,

I'm only too glad to receive
him and coach him.

Book VII, Chapter 8
To Transmit

不愤，不启；不悱，不
发。举一隅不以三隅
反，则不复也。

述而第七：八

I never enlighten anyone who is never driven to frustration by the urge to seek knowledge. **1**

Nor do I illuminate anyone who is never driven to frenzy by the urge to seek knowledge. **2**

3 When I have pointed out one corner of a square to him,

4 And he cannot make the connection with the other three, I will not teach him again.

105

Book VII,
Chapter 15
To Transmit

饭疏食，饮
水，曲肱而枕
之，乐亦在其
中矣。不义而
富且贵，于我
如浮云。
述而第七：十五

1 Eating nothing but plain rice,

2 Drinking nothing but plain water and,

3 Propping myself up on my arms can be such joy that...

4 Fortunes which do not come by the proper way are to me just passing clouds in the sky.

Book VII, Chapter 19
To Transmit

我非生而知之者；好古，敏以求之者也。

述而第七：
十九

1

I was not born with knowledge for everything.

2

It's just that I love to study ancient books,

3

And learn to understand them with an agile mind and hard work.

Book VII, Chapter 21
To Transmit

三人行，必有
我師焉。擇其
善者而從之；
其不善者而改
之。

述而第七：二一

When I'm walking in the company of two other men, there is always something I can learn from them...

1

Their strengths I pick up.

2

Their weakness I use for self-correction.

酒

Wine

3

Book VII,
Chapter 26
To Transmit

子钓而不纲;
弋不射宿。
述而第七: 二六

The Master fishes with a fishing rod,

But not with a large net,

He shoots with arrows.

But never shoots at roosting birds.

110

Book VII,
Chapter 36
To Transmit

子曰：「君子
坦荡荡，小人
长戚戚。」
述而第七：三六

The heart of a superior man is calm and serene...

Confucius said:

1

2

The heart of a petty man is fretful and ill at ease.

Are they gossiping about me again?

Book VIII, Chapter 4
Count Tai

曾子有疾，孟敬子问
之。曾子言曰：「鸟之
将死，其鸣也哀；人之
将死，其言也善。君子
所贵乎道者三；动容
貌，斯远暴慢矣；正颜
色，斯近信矣；出辞
气，斯远鄙倍矣。笾豆
之事，则有司存。」
泰伯第八：四

When Zeng Zi was ill, Meng Jing Zi came to see him. Zeng Zi said:

Wa!

Sad is the cry of a dying bird;

1

Kind are the words of a dying man.

2

There are three things in The Way which a gentleman values most:

3

To maintain a polite countenance in order to stay away from the boorish; to keep an honest expression in order to gain trust; to talk reasonably in order to avoid being senseless. As for sacrificial rites, there are officials responsible for them.

4

Book VIII, Chapter 7
Count Tai

曾子曰：「士不可以
不弘毅，任重而道
远。仁以为己任，不
亦重乎！死而后已，
不亦远乎！」

泰伯第八：七

Book VIII,
Chapter 17
Count Tai

学如不及，
犹恐失之。
泰伯第八：十七

There is so much to
catch up on in studies.

And whatever I have learned,
I'm afraid of losing.

Book IX, Chapter 16
Rarely Does the Master

逝者如斯夫!
不舍昼夜。
子罕第九: 十六

Is this how everything in life passes?

1

Day and night without a break.

2

Book IX, Chapter 22
Rarely Does the Master

后生可畏；焉知来者之不如今也？四
十五十而无闻焉，斯亦不足畏也已！

子罕第九：二二

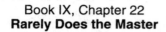

1

Young men should
not be underestimated.

2

How can we be
sure their future
would not be
brighter than
our present?

3

Still, if a man
achieves nothing
by the age of
forty or fifty,

4

Then there is
nothing about him
that is worthy of
our respect.

118

子曰：「三军
可夺帅也，匹
夫不可夺志
也。」
子罕第九：二五

Confucius said:
You may be able to overcome
the general of a great army;

But you cannot move
the firm will of a
common man.

119

Book IX, Chapter 28
Rarely Does the Master

知者不惑，仁者不忧，勇者不惧。

子罕第九：二八

The wise is never confused.

The benevolent is never worried.

The courageous is never afraid.

Book X, Chapter 11
At Home

厩焚。子退
朝，曰：「伤
人乎？」不问
马。

乡党第十：十一

Confucius' stables caught fire.

1

On returning from court, he asked:

2

Was anyone hurt?

He did not ask if the horses were hurt.

3

Book XI, Chapter 11
The Pioneers

季路问事鬼神? 子
曰: 「未能事人,
焉能事鬼? 」曰:
「敢问死? 」曰:
「未知生，焉知
死? 」

先进第十一: 十一

122

Book XI, Chapter 15
The Pioneers

子贡问：「师与商
也孰贤？」子曰：
「师也过，商也不
及。」曰：「然则
师愈与？」子曰：
「过犹不及。」

先进第十一：十五

123

Book XI,
Chapter 17
The Pioneers

柴也愚，参也
鲁，师也辟，由
也喭。回也其庶
乎！屡空。赐不
受命而货殖焉，
亿则屡中。

先进第十一：十七

1 Gao Chai is dull-witted.

2 Zeng Shen is slow,

3 Chuan Sun Shi is extroverted and lacks honesty,

4 Zhong You is aggressive.

5 Yan Hui has inclinations for scholarly achievement but his ambitions are often trapped by poverty!

6 Duan Mu Ci refuses to accept his lot and went into business. His speculations on prices are so accurate that he makes huge profits.

Book XII, Chapter 1
Yan Yuan

颜渊问仁。子曰：「克己复礼为仁。一日克己复礼，天下归仁焉。为仁由己，而由人乎哉？」颜渊曰：「请问其目？」子曰：「非礼勿视，非礼勿听、非礼勿言，非礼勿动。」颜渊曰：「回虽不敏，请事斯语矣！」

颜渊第十二：一

Yan Yuan asked:

What is benevolence?

To be able to overcome your desire and observe the rites in living. This is benevolence.

1

Benevolence is derived from self-discipline; it is not given by others.

When a man reaches such a state, the whole world should regard him a benevolent man.

2

Can you please list the items?

3

Do not look unless it accords with the rites;

Do not listen unless it accords with the rites;

Do not speak unless it accords with the rites;

Do not act unless it accords with the rites.

4

Although I am a little slow, I shall hope to practise what you have just told me.

5

125

Book XII, Chapter 2
Yan Yuan

仲弓问仁。子曰：「出门如见大宾，使民如承大祭。己所不欲，勿施于人。在邦无怨，在家无怨。」仲弓曰：「雍虽不敏，请事斯语矣！」
颜渊第十二：二

Zhong Gong asked about the constitution of a moral life.

When abroad, honour everyone as you would honour an important guest in your own home.

In employing the services of the common people, do it as if you are bearing the responsibility of an important sacrifice.

Do not do to others what you yourself would not like done unto you.

In your public or private life, give no one any reason to complain against you.

I know I'm not clever, but I'll try to put your words into practice.

Book XII, Chapter 5
Yan Yuan

司马牛忧曰：「人皆有兄弟，我独亡！」子夏曰：「商闻之矣："死生有命，富贵在天。"君子敬而无失，与人恭而有礼，四海之内，皆兄弟也。君子何患乎无兄弟也？」

颜渊第十二：五

1 A sorrowful Si Ma Niu said to Zi Xia:

All of you have brothers, I have none.

2

I have heard that life and death are a matter of Fate; riches and honour are determined by Heaven.

3

If a capable gentleman is reverent and does nothing wrong and treats people respectfully,

4 All within the Four Seas can be his brothers.

5

Why should a gentleman worry that he has no brothers?

Book XII, Chapter 7
Yan Yuan

子贡问政。子曰：「足食，足兵，民信之矣。」子贡曰：「必不得已而去，于斯三者何先？」曰：「去兵。」子贡曰：「必不得已而去，于斯二者何先？」曰：「去食。自古皆有死，民无信不立。」

颜渊第十二：七

Book XII,
Chapter 16
Yan Yuan

君子成人之
美，不成人之
恶；小人反
是。
颜渊第十二：十六

The gentleman
helps others to
utilise their
strengths and not
their weaknesses;

The petty man
does the opposite.

Book XII, Chapter 17 **Yan Yuan**

季康子问政于孔
子。孔子对曰:
「政者正也，子帅
以正，孰敢不
正? 」

颜渊第十二: 十七

Ji Kang asked Confucius about the art of government...

To govern means to put things right,

If you lead the people in an upright way, who will dare go a crooked way?

子貢問友。子曰：
「忠告而善道之，
不可則止，毋自辱
焉。」

顏淵第十二：二三

Book XII,
Chapter 24
Yan Yuan

曾子曰：「君子以
文会友；以友辅
仁。」

颜渊第十二：二四

1

Zeng Zi said:
A gentleman makes friends
through being cultured,

2

And looks to friends
to help him cultivate
benevolence.

子路问政。子
曰：「先之，劳
之。」请益。
曰：「无倦。」
子路第十三：一

Zi Lu asked
Confucius about
the art of
government...

1

Master, how
should one rule?

Lead the people by your
example; show them that
you're hardworking, and
the people will work
hard without complaint.

2

3

Anything else?

4

In your efforts to
do this, be not weary.

133

Book XIII,
Chapter 13
Zi Lu

苟正其身矣，于
从政乎何有？不
能正其身，如正
人何？

子路第十三：十三

If my conduct is upright, taking part in government will not be difficult for me.

If my conduct is not upright, how can I correct the misconduct of others?

135

Book XIII, Chapter 17
Zi Lu

子夏为莒父宰，问政。
子曰：「无欲速，无见
小利；欲速则不达，见
小利则大事不成。」

子路第十三：十七

1

Zi Xia became prefect of Ju Fu.

2

He sought advice from Confucius on the art of government.

3

Do not hope for quick results; do not see just petty gains.

4

If you want quick results, you can never complete your tasks.

5

And if you only see petty gains, you can never achieve great things.

樊迟问仁。子曰：「居
处恭，执事敬，与人
忠：虽之夷狄，不可弃
也。」

子路第十三：十九

Fan Ci asked
Confucius:

Master, how
should one live
a moral life?

1

Be humble in daily living, be
serious in business, and be
sincere in relationships.

2

3

Even if you should
live among
barbarians, you
cannot abandon
these principles.

Book XIII,
Chapter 23
Zi Lu

子曰：「君子和
而不同，小人同
而不和。」
子路第十三：二三

Book XIII, Chapter 26
Zi Lu

子曰：「君子泰
而不驕，小人驕
而不泰。」
子路第十三：二六

139

Book XIV, Chapter 1
Xian Enquires

宪问耻。子曰：
「邦有道，谷；邦
无道，谷，耻
也。」

宪问第十四：一

1 Yuan Xian asked about the meaning of 'shame'.

Shame?

2 'Shame' means to draw a salary without making contributions when the state is run properly,

3 Or without cultivating oneself when the state is in disarray.

4 All that is shameful!

子曰：「贫而无
怨，难；富而无
骄，易。」
宪问第十四：十一

Book XIV, Chapter 13
Xian Enquires

子路问成人。子曰：「若臧武仲之知，公绰之不欲，卞庄子之勇，冉求之艺；文之以礼乐，亦可为成人矣！」曰：「今之成人者，何必然？见利思义，见危授命，久要不忘平生之言，亦可以为成人矣！」

宪问第十四：十三

1 Zi Lu asked:

What makes a complete man?

2 A man as intelligent as Zang Wu Zhong,

3 As free from greed as Meng Gong Chuo,

4 As courageous as Zhuang Zi of Bian,

5 As talented as Ran Qiu and is well-versed in the rites and music. These qualities make a complete man.

6 But nowadays to be a complete man, one need not have all these qualities. If you remember what is right at the sight of benefit, is ready to die in times of danger and never forget to keep old promises, you may be considered a complete man.

142

其言之不怍，
则为之也难!
宪问第十四：二一

143

Book XIV, Chapter 21
Xian Enquires

子曰：「其言之
不怍，则为之也
难！」

宪问第十四：二一

For a man to have
nothing to be ashamed
of and nothing to hide,

1

It means putting
his daily conduct to severe tests.

2

Book XIV,
Chapter 25
**Xian
Enquires**

子曰：「古之
学者为己，今
之学者为人。」
宪问第十四：二五

Confucius
said:

In the old days, men sought
knowledge in order to
improve themselves;

1

2

Nowadays,
men seek knowledge
to impress other
people.

**Book XIV,
Chapter 29
Xian Enquires**

君子耻其言而
过其行。

宪问第十四：二九

The gentleman is careful
not to commit himself
in word,

I'll try
my best.

But does so in deed.

He's productive
and good.

Book XIV, Chapter 31
Xian Enquires

子貢方人。子
曰：「賜也，
賢乎哉？夫我
則不暇！」

憲問第十四：三一

147

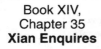

Book XIV,
Chapter 35
Xian Enquires

骥不称其力，
称其德。
宪问第十四：三五

A good horse is
praised not for
its power.

But for its tameness.

Book XIV, Chapter 36
Xian Enquires

或曰：「以德报
怨，何如？」子
曰：「何以德报？
以直报怨，以德报
德。」

宪问第十四：三六

Book XIV, Chapter 37
Xian Enquires

子曰：「莫我知也夫！」子
貢曰：「何为其莫知子
也?」子曰：「不怨天，不
尤人，下学而上达：知我
者，其天乎！」

宪问第十四：三七

子路宿于石门。晨门
曰：「奚自？」子路
曰：「自孔氏。」曰：
「是知其不可而为之者
与？」

宪问第十四：四一

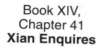

Zi Lu stayed one night outside the Stone Gate.

Hello!

The gatekeeper came up to him.

Where did you come from?

I came from the Kong family.

Is that the Kong who is bent on working towards a goal he knows he can never achieve?

Book XIV, Chapter 46
Xian Enquires

原壤夷俟。子曰：「幼
而不孫弟，長而無述
焉，老而不死是為
賊！」以杖叩其脛。

憲問第十四：四六

1

When Yuan Rang, Confucius'
old friend saw him coming,
he squatted down on the ground
to wait for him.

2 When you were young,
you were neither modest
nor filial.

3 When you grew up,
you did nothing
worthwhile,

4 And now you are old,
you refuse to die.
You are a pest
indeed!

5 So said, the Master tapped
him on the shin with a
walking stick.

Book XV,
Chapter 6
Duke Ling of Wei

直哉史鱼！邦有道，如矢；
邦无道，如矢。君子哉蘧伯
玉！邦有道，则仕；邦无
道，则可卷而怀之。

卫灵公第十五：六

1
What an upright character
Shi Yu is! When the state
is run orderly, he serves it
loyally and is as straight
as an arrow;

2
When the state is in disarray,
he offers frank advice and is still
as straight as an arrow.

When a gentleman Qu Po Yu is!
When the state is run orderly,
he takes office,

When the state is in disarray,
he retreats, withholding
his talent.

3

4

153

Book XV,
Chapter 7
Duke Ling of Wei

子曰：「可与言，而
不与之言，失人；不可
与言，而与
之言，失言。
知者不失人，
亦不失言。」
卫灵公第
十五：七

1

Not speaking with a man who can be spoken to, is to have missed and lost a man.

2

Speaking with those who cannot be spoken to, is to have wasted one's words.

3

Those who are wise do not lose their man nor waste their words.

Book XV,
Chapter 9
**Duke Ling
of Wei**

子贡问仁。子
曰：「工欲善
其事，必先利
其器。居是邦
也，事其大夫
之贤者，友其
士之仁者。」
卫灵公第十五：九

1 If the craftsman wants to do a good job, he must first sharpen his tools.

Zi Gong asked about the cultivation of benevolence.

2 In whatever state you live, you should work for a capable government,

3 And make friends with benevolent gentlemen.

155

Book XV,
Chapter 11
Duke Ling of Wei

人无远虑，
必有近忧。
卫灵公第十五：十一

A man who does not think
far ahead in whatever he does,

Is sure to be troubled by
worries much closer at hand.

Book XV,
Chapter 16
**Duke Ling
of Wei**

子曰：「群居终日，言
不及义，好行小慧，难
矣哉！」
卫灵公第十五：十六

Confucius said: 1

When men
getting together for a
whole day speak nothing
of what is right or true,
but are content with smart
talk and acts of petty
cleverness,

Then theirs is a
hard case, because
nothing good can be
made of them.

2

Book XV, Chapter 22 **Duke Ling of Wei**

子曰：「君子不以言舉，人，不以人廢言。」
衛靈公第十五：二二

The superior man does not promote a man because of what he says;

He speaks well; let's make him an official!

1

2

Nor reject his valuable sayings because of who he is.

But he is not worthy...

Book XV, Chapter 23
Duke Ling of Wei

子贡问曰：「有一言而
可以终身行之者乎？」
子曰：「其恕乎！己所
不欲，勿施于人。」
卫灵公第十五：二三

1

Zi Gong asked:

Is there a word that can serve as the basic principle of conduct throughout the whole life?

恕
Shu

2

It may be the word 'Shu'.*

恕
Shu

3

Do not impose on others,

4

What you yourself do not like.

* forbearance

159

Book XV,
Chapter 28
**Duke Ling
of Wei**

子曰：「人能弘
道，非道弘人。」
卫灵公第十五：二八

162

Book XV,
Chapter 30
**Duke Ling
of Wei**

吾尝终日不食，
终夜不寝，以思；
无益，不如学也。
卫灵公第十五：三十

164

Book XV,
Chapter 36
**Duke Ling
of Wei**

子曰：「君子貞而
不諒。」
衛靈公第十五：三六

166

167

Book XVI, Chapter 7
Ji Family

君子有三戒：少之时，血气
未定，戒之在色；及其壮
也，血气方刚，戒之在斗；
及其老也，血气既衰，戒之
在得。

季氏第十六：七

There are three things that the gentleman should guard against: When he is young, his blood and *qi** are unstable, he must guard against sexual desires.

1

In his prime, his blood and *qi* are at their peak, he must guard against bellicosity.**

2

At old age, his blood and *qi* have declined, so he must guard against excessive greed.

3

* the basic component of the universe. It fills the human body and circulates with the blood.
** to be war-like by nature.

168

Book XVI, Chapter 9
Ji Family

孔子曰：「生而知
之者，上也；学而
知之者，次也；困
而学之，又其次
也；困而不学，民
斯为下矣！」

季氏第十六：九

Confucius said:

The highest class of men are those who are born with a natural understanding;

1

Next are those who readily acquire understanding by study;

2

3
Then there are those who have to toil laboriously to acquire understanding;

Finally, the lowest class of men are those who are naturally dull but yet will not labour to acquire understanding.

4

169

Book XVI, Chapter 10
Ji Family

君子有九思：
视思明，听思聪，
色思温，貌思恭，
言思忠，事思敬，
疑思问，忿思难，
见得思义。
季氏第十六：十

There are nine things
which the gentleman
should ponder upon: 1

When looking,
he must think
of seeing clearly. 2

When hearing, he must 3
think of hearing clearly.

When expressing his 4
moods, he must look
amicable,

Behaving in a 5
courteous manner.

Honesty... 6

When
speaking,
he must
think of
honesty.

When working, he must 7
think of giving his best.

When in doubt, he must 8
think of questioning.

When showing 9
his anger, he must
think of the
consequences.

When he sees a benefit, 10
he must ponder whether
he deserves it.

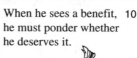

Book XVI, Chapter 12
Ji Family

诚不以富，亦祇以异。
齐景公有马千驷，死之
日，民无德而称焉。伯
夷、叔齐饿于首阳之
下，民到于今称之。其
斯之谓与？

季氏第十六：十二

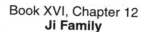

The Odes (*Shi Jing*) says that a man should be praised not because of his wealth but because of his superior conduct.

1

Duke Jing of Qi owned 4,000 horses but when he died, the people found nothing praiseworthy about him.

2

3

Although Bo Yi and Shu Qi starved to death at the foot of Mount Shou Yang, to this day, people are still praising them. That must be what The Odes are referring to.

171

Book XVII, Chapter 2
Yang Huo

性相近也，
习相远也。
阳货第十七：二

All men are alike by nature.

But because of differences in education and environment,

Their differences become more and more apparent.

Book XVII, Chapter 8
Yang Huo

子曰：「由也，女闻六言六蔽矣乎？」对曰：「未也。」「居！吾语女：好仁不好学，其蔽也愚；好知不好学，其蔽也荡；好信不好学，其蔽也贼；好直不好学，其蔽也绞；好勇不好学，其蔽也乱；好刚不好学，其蔽也狂。」

阳货第十七：八

Have you heard about the six flaws said to be associated with the six merits?

No, I haven't.

Confucius asked Zhong You:

1

Sit down, let me tell you.

Yes, Master.

2

To love benevolence without loving learning may lead to ignorance;
to love cleverness without loving learning may lead to misconduct;
to love honesty without loving learning may lead to harm;
to love uprightness without loving learning may lead to rashness;
to love courage without loving learning may lead to misfortunes and finally,
to love mightiness without loving learning may lead to brashness.

3

173

Book XVII,
Chapter 12
Yang Huo

色厉而内荏，
譬诸小人，
其犹穿窬之
盗也与！

阳货第十七：
十二

1

A man who looks imposing on the outside...

2

But who is deep down a coward...

3

Is, when likened to a small man...

4

Similar to the burglar who breaks in or climbs over walls. How shameful he is!

Book XVII, Chapter 13
Yang Huo

子曰：「乡愿，
德之贼也！」
阳货第
十七：十三

Confucius said:

Book XVII, Chapter 14
Yang Huo

子曰：
「道听
而途说，
德之弃
也！」
阳货第十七：
十四

Confucius said:

176

Book XVII, Chapter 15
Yang Huo

子曰：「鄙夫！可与事
君也与哉？其未得之
也，患得之。既得之，
患失之；苟患失之，无
所不至矣！」

阳货第十七：十五

Panel 1

Confucius said:

Those despicable creatures! How could one possibly serve the country in the company of such men?

Panel 2

These men maintain only selfish interests;

How can I make things better for myself...

Panel 3

Before they attain an official position, they think and worry only about how they can get it.

Please put in a good word for me...

Panel 4

After they've attained an official position, their sole anxiety is losing it.

Panel 5

And in their anxiety that they may lose it, there is nothing they will not do!

I'll destroy anyone who would touch my position!

177

Book XVII,
Chapter 18
Yang Huo

子曰：「恶紫之夺朱
也，恶郑声之乱雅乐也，
恶利口之覆邦家者。」

阳货第十七：
十八

Book XVII,
Chapter 20
Yang Huo

孺悲欲见孔子，孔子辞
以疾。将命者出户，取
瑟而歌，使之闻之。
阳货第十七：二十

1 Ru Bei wanted to see Confucius.

2 Tell him I'm sick, I can't see him.

Yes, Master.

3 Sorry, my master is sick. He cannot see you.

4

5 Confucius took out his lute and started singing aloud so that Ru Bei could hear him.

6 How disgusting! You are not sick at all.

179

**Book XVII,
Chapter 22
Yang Huo**

饱食终日，
无所用心：
难矣哉！
不有博弈者乎？
为之犹贤乎已！
阳货第十七：二二

1

A man who idles around
after he has filled his stomach,

2

Will not have
any achievement at all,

wine

3

Aren't there such games as the
board game and *Wei Qi**?
Even having a go at them is
better than doing nothing
the whole day.

* a kind of Chinese chess

180

Book XVII,
Chapter 25
Yang Huo

唯女子与小人难养也。
近之则不逊，远之则
怨。
阳货第十七：二五

1
The maids and servants
of the household are the
most difficult to handle.

2
If you get too close to them,
they become insolent.

3
Go away!
How rude
you are!

If you keep a distance,
they will complain.

4
Huh! Our
master looks
down on us
servants.

181

Book XVII,
Chapter 26
Yang Huo

年四十而见
恶焉，其终
也已！
阳货第十七：
二六

1

Get lost!

If, by the age of forty,
a man still displays wicked
behaviour,

2

Do not expect anything good
to come out of him for
the rest of his life.

182

Book XVIII, Chapter 1
The Viscount of Wei

微子去之，箕子為之奴，比干諫
而死。孔子曰：「殷有三仁焉！」
微子第十八：一

Shang Zhou, king of the Yin Dynasty, was such a despot that his brother, the Viscount of Wei, left him.

1

His uncle, the Viscount of Ji, was imprisoned as a slave for remonstrating with him,

2

And another uncle Bi Gan was killed for the same reason.

3

There were three men of benevolence who lived at the end of the Yin Dynasty.

Confucius commented in awe:

4

Book XVIII, Chapter 5
The Viscount of Wei

楚狂接輿，歌而过孔
子，曰：「凤兮！凤
兮！何德之衰？往者
不可谏，来者犹可
追。已而！已而！今
之从政者殆而！」孔
子下，欲与之言；趋
而辟之，不得与之
言。

微子第十八：五

Jie Yu, the lunatic of Chu,
passed by Confucius'
chariot, singing:

1

Phoenix, oh phoenix!
How thy virtue has decayed!
What is past is beyond redemption.
What is to come is not yet gone.

Let it be! Let it be!
Perilous is the fate of
those in government!

3

Confucius got off his chariot
to talk to him; but he was gone in
a flash and there was no chance
for a discussion.

4

Book XVIII, Chapter 6
The Viscount of Wei

长沮、桀溺耦而耕。孔子过之，使子路问津焉。
长沮曰：「夫执舆者为谁？」子路曰：「为孔
丘。」曰：「是鲁孔丘与？」曰：「是也。」
曰：「是知津矣！」问于桀溺，桀溺曰：「子为
谁？」曰：「为仲由。」曰：「是鲁孔丘之徒
与？」对曰：「然。」曰：「滔滔者，天下皆是
也；而谁以易之？且而与其从辟人之士也，岂若
从辟世之士哉？」耰而不辍。子路行以告。夫子
怃然曰：「鸟兽不可与同群，吾非斯人之徒与而
谁与？天下有道，丘不与易也。」

微子第十八：六

1 Chang Ju and Jie Ni were ploughing in the field when Confucius passed by in his chariot.

2 Go and ask them where the ford is.

Yes, Master.

Can you please tell me where the ford is?

3 Who's the man holding the reins?

187

188

Book XIX, Chapter 9
Zi Zhang

子夏曰：「君子有
三变：望之俨然，
即之也温，听其言
也厉。」

子张第十九：九

1

Zi Xia said:

"A gentleman always gives others three different impressions: From afar, he appears stately,

2

On a closer look, he appears amiable,

3

But when he speaks, he sounds stern."

191

Book XIX, Chapter 10
Zi Zhang

子夏曰：「君子信而后劳其民；未信，则以为厉己也。信而后谏；未信，则以为谤己也。」

子张第十九：十

Zi Xia said:

A superior official must first win the confidence of the people before he can put them to work.

Otherwise, they will think that he is oppressing them.

You're abusing us!

Besides, he must win the confidence of his sovereign before he can venture to point out his errors.

Otherwise, the sovereign will think that he is being slandered.

How dare you malign me!

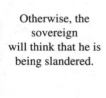

192

Book XIX, Chapter 11
Zi Zhang

子夏曰：「大
德不踰閑，
小德出入可
也。」
子张第十九：
十一

Zi Xia said:

As long as a man does not transgress moral principles of great importance,

1

He may trespass in the minor points of moral conduct.

2

193

Book XIX, Chapter 13
Zi Zhang

子夏曰：「仕
而優則學，學
而優則仕。」

子張第十九：
十三

1

Zi Xia said:

"When a man is able to cope beyond official duties, he should devote more time to studies.

2

When a scholar is able to cope beyond studies, he should take office,

3

So as to serve his country and his people."

**Book XIX, Chapter 21
Zi Zhang**

子贡曰：「君
子之过也，如
日月之食焉；
过也，人皆见
之；更也，人
皆仰之。」

子张第十九：
二一

Zi Gong said:
The gentleman's errors are
like an eclipse of the sun
and moon; when he errs,
the whole world can see it.

When he corrects himself,
the whole world
looks up to him.

Book XX, Chapter 3
Yao Speaks

不知命，无以为君子也；
不知礼，无以立也；不知
言，无以知人也。
尧曰第二十：三

1

A man who does not know
the will of Heaven cannot
be a gentleman;

A man who knows nothing
about the rites cannot establish
himself in society.

2

A man who cannot tell right
from wrong is unable to
tell good men from the evil.

3

Confucius' Pupils

198

Yan Hui 颜回

Yan Hui styled himself Zi Yuan.
He was a native of Lu and was younger
than Confucius by thirty years.

1 Yan Hui's hair turned grey when he was only twenty-nine. He passed away at the age of thirty-two.

2 When he died, Confucius could not stop weeping.

Alas! There will be no one to succeed me. I'm finished! I'm finished!

3 Master, please take care and don't be overgrieved.

4 Am I overgrieved? Whom shall I grieve for if not for Yan Hui?

Min Sun 闵损

Min Sun styled himself Zi Qian.
He was a native of Lu and was younger
than Confucius by fifteen years.

---

1 Confucius once praised him.
"What a filial son Min Zi Qian is.
He serves and obeys his parents
and loves his brothers,

2 So much so that there is no
way anyone can reproach
him in front of his parents
and brothers."

3 A man of principle, he once
declined an offer by the powerful
Ji family to be their steward and
would not accept employment
from corrupt princes. To the
messenger sent by the Ji family,
he said:

4 If anyone comes to ask
for me again, tell them I
shall be on the other side
of the River Wen.

Ran Yong 冉雍

Ran Yong styled himself Zhong Gong.
He was a native of Lu and was younger than
Confucius by twenty-nine years.
He came from a poor family for his father
belonged to the lowest rung of society.

1

A bull may be born of plough cattle, yet as long as his coat has a clear colour and his horns are well-shaped, he is fit to be used as sacrificial bull.

2

Even though man may find him unsuitable because of his inferior stock,

3

The spirits of the mountains and rivers surely wouldn't want to give him up.

Zhong You 仲由

Zhong You, styled Zi Lu, was a native of Bian and was younger than Confucius by nine years. He used to be a boorish, hearty man who loved muscles and might, but eventually mellowed through the influence of Confucius. In his old age, Zi Lu served as Counsellor of Pu of Wei. He was killed in a revolt in Wei.

Who else but Zhong You can stand beside a man garbed in fur coat, himself in old robes, without feeling embarrassed?

In learning, Zhong You has certainly reached the grand hall of enlightenment, only that he hasn't quite penetrated the depths of the inner chambers yet.

1

2

202

Zai Yu 宰予

Zai Yu styled himself Zi Wo. A native of Lu, Zai Yu was an eloquent man well-versed in the art of debate. He was Counsellor of Lin Zi of Qi and was involved in a revolt staged by Tian Chang. Because of him, his whole family was implicated and killed, leaving Confucius to lament deeply for him.

203

Duan Mu Ci
端木賜

Duan Mu Ci, styled Zi Gong, was a native of Wei and was younger than Confucius by thirty-one years. He was eloquent and a good debater who loved to spread the faults as much as the strengths of others.

On more than one occasion, he has helped Lu and Wei out of dire straits. He was wealthy and possessed a business acumen, which earned him fortunes. He died of old age in Qi.

Bu Shang

卜商

Bu Shang, styled Zi Xia, was a native of Wen and was younger than Confucius by forty-five years. After the Master had passed away, Zi Xia went and settled in Xi He of Wei, where he recruited pupils and became a teacher of Duke Wen of Wei. When his son died, he cried so hard that he became blind.

1 Zi Xia asked: The Odes says: *"Her delightful smiles are rippling, Her beautiful eyes are glancing, Colours are painted on plain silk."* What is the meaning of these three lines?

2 It means that when you paint, you have white as a base and then put colours on it.

3 It may mean that man must possess virtue first and then refine it with the practice of rites. Is that correct?

4 What you have said has enlightened me on the poem. It looks like I can only discuss The Odes with someone as bright as you are.

205

Tantai Mie Min 澹台灭明

Tantai Mie Ming styled himself Zi Yu. He was a native of Wu Cheng and was younger than Confucius by thirty-nine years. Zi Yu, though ugly, was an upright and honest man. In later years, he travelled to the states south of the Yangtzu River, where he recruited some three hundred students. He set up personal guidelines on give-and-take and observed them strictly. For this, his integrity spread widely among the lords.

1 Zi You was a steward of Wu Cheng.

2 Is there any virtuous man over there who can assist you?

3 There is this man called Tantai Mie Ming who does things according to the law and never takes short-cuts.

4 He never comes to my place except on official business.

Yuan Xian

原宪

Yuan Xian styled himself Zi Si and was a native of Lu. He was very poor and after the Master died, he went away to live by a remote river.

207

Zhuan Sun Shi

颛孙师

Zhuan Sun Shi, styled Zi Zhang, was a native of Chen and was younger than Confucius by forty-eight years. Zi Zhang was meticulous with attire and preoccupied with a stately presentation. For this reason, Zeng Zi once said of him: It is difficult to practise virture in the company of a man like this.

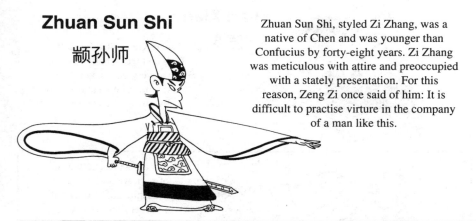

1 Zi Zhang wanted to know how he could acquire an official post.

Listen widely to what people say to enrich yourself. Whatever you doubt, you can leave out but whatever you don't, repeat cautiously. In this way, there will be few mistakes.

Observe widely how people handle matters. What you don't feel right, don't do it.

But whatever you do, do it cautiously.

2

In this way, you will have few regrets and make few mistakes in your words and deeds. When that is achieved,

3

4 An official post will come your way.

Zeng Shen

曾参

Zeng Shen styled himself Zi Yu. He was a native of Nan Wu Cheng of Lu and was younger than Confucius by forty-six years. The Master felt he could understand filial piety thoroughly and so made him his pupil. Zeng Shen wrote a book entitled *"Xiao* Jing"*. He died in his old age in Lu.

* *Xiao* means 'filial'.

Fan Xu
樊须

Fan Xu, styled Zi Chi, was a native of Qi and was younger than Confucius by thirty-six years.

You Ruo

有若

You Ruo, styled Zi You, was a native of Lu and was younger than Confucius by forty-three years. After Confucius died, his pupils missed him badly and because You Ruo resembled the Master in appearance, they made him their teacher.

* 和 means 'harmony'.   ** 礼 means 'rites'.

Gong Ye Zhang

公冶长

Gong Ye Zhang, styled Zi Zhang,
was a native of Qi and
was Confucius' son-in-law.

This man Zi Zhang is good enough to be one's son-in-law. Although he was imprisoned, he was really not responsible for the crime.

1

And Confucius offered his daughter's hand to him in marriage.

2

Nan Gong Gua 南宫括

Nan Gong Gua, styled Zi Rong,
was a native of Lu.
Confucius had this to say about him:
"When the government was orderly, he did not
have to lose his office, and when the government
was topsy-turvy, he managed to keep
clear of trouble." And Confucius offered his
brother's daughter to him in marriage.

1. Yi excelled in archery, while Ao excelled in canoeing. Both were men of courage, but they died terrible deaths.

2. Xia Yu and Hou Ji were different. They took to ploughing the fields themselves and still ruled the world. Wasn't that true?

3. Since Confucius offered no answer, Zi Rong excused himself.

4. What a gentleman he is! What a follower of benevolence!

Gong Xi Chi

公西赤

Gong Xi Chi, styled Zi Hua, was a native of Lu and was younger than Confucius by forty-two years.

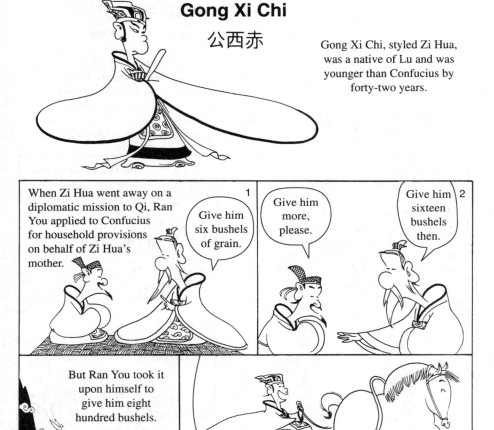

When Zi Hua went away on a diplomatic mission to Qi, Ran You applied to Confucius for household provisions on behalf of Zi Hua's mother.

Give him six bushels of grain.

1

Give him more, please.

Give him sixteen bushels then.

2

But Ran You took it upon himself to give him eight hundred bushels.

When Confucius knew about it, he said:

When Gong Xi Chi went away on a diplomatic mission to Qi, he was riding in a chariot drawn by well-fed horses and dressed in fine warm clothes. I have heard that a gentleman seeks to help others in need, not to increase his own fortunes.

3

4

EPILOGUE

On the death of Confucius, Zi Gong suggested that all the disciples should observe the traditional three-year mourning period to express their gratitude to their teacher.

When the three years were up, some of the disciples stayed on near the tomb, while others left, having said goodbye to one another.

2

At that time, there was a great demand for talented men, so the disciples were able to spread the teachings of Confucius in different places.

3

Zi Xia went to the court of the princes of Wei and took on the responsibility of educating them in the Confucian Way. He was later known as Transmitter of the Classical Books.

1

Zeng Zi stayed on and devoted himself to work on expanding the teachings of Confucius. Later generations called him Explicator of the Fundamental Principles of the Sage.

2

Besides his disciples, many natives of Lu also came to live near Confucius' tomb, and in time, a village known as Kong's Village was formed there.

3

Confucius' home was turned into a temple, and within were kept many of his personal belongings. The Temple later became a sacred place for scholars who desired to follow the Confucian Way.

4

217

Zeng Zi, making good use of this conducive environment, gathered there many young men of Lu and began the work of teaching and spreading the Confucian Way.

1

3

Zeng Zi, Zi You and Zi Xia varied in their explication of Confucius' teachings. Zi You and Zi Xia emphasized rituals, the sense of propriety and the practical aspects of government...

While Zeng Zi emphasized the conscience of the individual, his faithfulness, generosity, sincerity and trustworthiness.

2

Eventually, the Teaching of Confucius was handed down by Zeng Zi to Zi Si, Confucius' grandson, and after his death, to Mencius through his disciples.

Zeng Zi

Zi Si

Mencius

SPECIAL OFFER

Romance of the Three Kingdoms Vols. 1-10 in a NEW DISPLAY BOX!
China's Greatest Historical Classics in Comics

***FREE: 216-page comics entitled "Sixteen Strategies of Zhuge Liang".
Free delivery.***

Offer for Local Readers:
Original Price for 10 volumes   **S$99.91** (*inclusive of* GST)
*Special price for whole kit   **S$97.00** (*inclusive of* GST)

Send this complete page for your mail order

I wish to order _____ set(s) *of Romance of the Three Kingdoms **Vol. 1-10***

at the nett price of S$97.00 per kit.

Enclosed is my postal order/money order/cheque No. _____

for S$ _____

Name _____ **Tel** _____

Address _____

_____ Singapore _____

Send to: ASIAPAC BOOKS PTE LTD 629 Aljunied Road #04-06 Cititech Industrial Building
Singapore 389838 Tel: 7453868 Fax: 7453822

Note: Prices are subject to change without prior notice. ***Offer is for readers in Singapore only.***

《亞太漫畫系列》

仁者的叮嚀

孔子説

編著：蔡志忠

亞太圖書有限公司出版